Borrowed Words

cut-up poems

by Peter Wortsman

BAMBOO DART PRESS

LOS ANGELES † NEW YORK † LONDON † MELBOURNE

Borrowed Words by Peter Wortsman

978-1-947240-57-5   Paperback
978-1-947240-58-2   eBook

First Printing 2022

Cover art by Harold Wortsman

Layout and design by Peter Wortsman and Mark Givens

For information:

Bamboo Dart Press

chapbooks@bamboodartpress.com

Bamboo Dart Press 026

Pelekinesis
www.pelekinesis.com

BAMBOO DART PRESS
www.bamboodartpress.com

SHRIMPER
www.shrimperrecords.com

THIS Book IS MADE WITH 100% RECYCLED language

"Wir spielen bis uns der Tod abholt."
(We play till death drags us away.)

Kurt Schwitters

Contents

Foreword

Language is a limited resource. Contrary to the commonly held conviction, the reservoir of speech is forever on the verge of drying up, or worse, calcifying into cliché. Like a farmer rotating his crops, I periodically plough words back into the mulch of meaning. Romanian émigré DADA poet Tristan Tzara (aka Samuel Rosenstock, 1896-1963) gave it a name: cut-up (or *découpé* in French). He revealed his original prescription in a text titled "How to Make a Dada Poem."[1]

I revert to cut-ups when I'm too distracted, depressed, dumbfounded or deranged to write in the regular manner. My sources include newspaper articles, sacred and profane texts, assorted print ads, packaging copy, and pretty much any other reading matter that comes to hand. In lieu of computer keyboard, pen and ink, my primary instruments are a razor blade, scissors, tweezers, and

---

[1]   "Take a newspaper./Take a pair of scissors./Select an article the length of/the poem you intend to compose./Cut out the article./Take care next to cut up/each of the words in the article/and put them in a bag./ Shake gently./Then remove each severed word/one after another./Copy them out conscientiously/in the order in which they emerged from the bag./The poem will resemble its maker./And there you are, an author of infinite originality/and a charming sensibility, although misunderstood/ by the mob." (The translation from the French is my own.)

glue. With little or no initial conscious intent, I skim the source text vertically and let my eye idle down the page, thereafter circling, cutting out, or copying seemingly random words and word combinations that strike my fancy. Telling snippets come together by what I call magnetic imminence.

As the isolation of virtual lockdown during the seemingly interminable Covid-19 pandemic stretches into its third year, I feel increasingly cut off from the word – a telling Freudian slip: I meant to write the *world*. Both are true. These days the words run ragged, like misfired fireworks, often exploding before they hit the page. A modern-day monk languishing in the solitude of my cell, I long for meaningful communion. But absent belief in a transcendent being, cut-ups take the place of prayer.

Initially I worked quickly, believing in the virtues of the haphazard. Cutting and pasting shreds of text with an experimental haste, I ignored glue splotches, misshapen letters, and bits of broken type. But what began as a game of verbal solitaire never intended for publication inevitably evolved into a method. In time I became more careful, more conscious of and conscientious in placement, concerned by the look as well as the content. Contrary to the timeworn adage, "You can't teach an old dog new tricks," my daughter, Aurélie, son, Jacques, and brother, Harold, coached me in the rudiments of computer design. And on the advice of my two most trusted readers, my wife, Claudie, and brother, Harold, I opted to preserve the raw originals as artifacts and present them side by side with the edited transcriptions. The reader is asked to consider the transcriptions the way one might poetic translations juxtaposed with the original words in certain books of foreign verse. My method can be summed up by one of the shortest texts in the collection: "On a wrinkled sheet of lined paper/my truest essence/an assemblage of/wrestling words."

Peter Wortsman
New York, May 1, 2021

almost a meditation.

On a wrinkled sheet of lined paper

my truest essence

an assemblage of

wrestling
       words

MAY 2, 2021

Almost a Meditation

On a wrinkled sheet of lined paper

my truest essence,

an assemblage of

wrestling

words.

May 2, 2021

the way the words look on the page.

A piece of crumpled
                parchment

        a floating blip

    aloof, disinterested

            bonsai

                body language

                    the same
                    dreaming
                            finger

            letters—

                'do not lie awake

                        signs
                    still seeking

                    secrets

        I THINK I'VE DISCOVERED

            The Dead Sea Scrolls,

                        MARCH 17, 2021

The Way the Words Look on the Page

A piece of crumpled
                    parchment,
        a floating blip
aloof, disinterested,
        bonsai
                body language —
                        the same
                        dreaming
                                finger
—letters
                do not lie awake —
                signs
        still seeking
                        secrets –
I think I've discovered
        The Dead Sea Scrolls.

March 17, 2021

'Nothing is normal these days.'

The convoluted strings of letters, numbers and dots

look oddly like

time slots

something other than

the rigid structures that had defined their days

"Everybody travels so fast that they don't get a chance to slow down,"

No one wants to talk about death.

MARCH 8, 2021

Nothing is Normal These Days

The convoluted strings of letters,
numbers and dots
look oddly
like time slots,
something other than
the rigid struc-
tures that had defined their days;
everybody travels so fast
they don't get a chance to slow down –
no one wants to talk
about death.

March 8, 2021

It Doesn't Disturb
The Dead at All

Sometimes the dancers hide their eyes, sometimes they stop their ears, sometimes they utter silent screams.

soundless laughter

Last week, the Pope startled several thouand listeners gathered for his weekly audience by insisting that angels exist.

which are unseen." the Pope said.

"They play like robots. You never know what they're thinking. But we play with heart."

It's a perfect hybrid.

Like shamanistic medieval tricksters,

"I've never believed in eternity, but I'm beginning to have my doubts.

It Doesn't Disturb the Dead at All

Sometimes the dancers hide their eyes,
sometimes they stop their ears,
sometimes they utter silent screams,
soundless laughter.

> Last week the Pope startled several thousand
> listeners gathered for his weekly audience by
> insisting that angels exist,
> which are unseen, the Pope said.

They play like robots,
you never know what they're thinking,
but we play with heart.

> It's a perfect hybrid,

> like shamanistic medieval tricksters.

> I've never believed in
> eternity, but I'm beginning to have
> my doubts.

February 19, 2021

Finding truth in

memory

time

welas
totems

looted

— angels, ancestors —

precariously, looming

"It's not fully my will."

It's up to the viewer
to fit the pieces together and sort
out meanings.

Real or imagined,

memory
stair is

snatches of

imponderables

"noise"

thought

silence.

longing

MARCH 5, 2021

Finding Truth in Memory

Time

welds

totems

—angels, ancestors—

precariously looming;

it's not fully my will,

real or imagined;

memory

stains

snatches of

imponderables:

noise,

thoughts,

silence,

longing.

March 5, 2021

**where the
silence is**

something about the quiet,

the trancelike
indiscriminate

trying to find words for things there aren't
words for,"

Like budding flowers awakening

APRIL 9, 2021

Where the Silence Is

Something about the quiet,

the trancelike

indiscriminate,

trying to find words for things

there aren't words for,

like budding flowers awakening.

April 9, 2021

silence
wanted
sound

— a hymn —

You never

stop being assailed.

in the subways,

on the streets,

a blaring car horn

horny pigeons jostling

against the backdrop of
conversation

people unspooled

I used to avoid noise,

but

something shifted

listening to

Italians singing from
their balconies

There's something about that
release.

The song is there,
and you can take off anywhere."

MARCH 14, 2021

Silence
Wanted
Sound

—a hymn—

You never
stop being assailed
in the subway,
on the streets,
a blaring car horn,
horny pigeons jostling
against the backdrop
of conversation:
people unspooled;
I used to avoid noise,
but
something shifted,
listening to
Italians singing
from their balconies;
there's something about that release,
the song is there
and you can take it anywhere.

March 14, 2021

The song itself

an "Ur-melodie"

in lyrical
solos

agonized vocals —

RAW
utterances,

piercing,
dissonant

a voice,
makes it onto the page.

It's a wary voice,

si-
multaneously focused and deranged.

invisible
lips

kiss
my ear

Sometimes, we hear words

sometimes the silence is just as

electric

APRIL 22, 2021

The Song Itself

An Ur-melodie
in lyrical
solos,
agonized vocals
—raw
utterances,
piercing,
dissonant –
a voice
makes it onto the page;
it's a wary voice,
si-
multaneously focused and deranged;
invisible lips
kiss
my ear;
sometimes we hear words,
sometimes the silence is just as
electric.

April 22, 2021

Dream song

New York,
the echoing skyline

broken stalagmites,
traces of fire and burned bones.

potential future archaeological find.   a

even more ephemeral than
actual ephemera.

watching the rain fall on the empty

streets

tears talking

the pretext, not the point.

overshadowed by
mind

I don't exist.

Wouldn't it be
nice if we could all wake up now?

MARCH 18, 2021

Dream Song

New York,
the echoing skyline:

broken stalagmites,
traces of fire and burned bones,
a potential future archeological find,

even more ephemeral
than actual ephemera

—watching the rain fall on the empty streets—

tears talking,
the pretext, not the point,
overshadowed by
mind.

I don't exist.

Wouldn't it be nice
if we could all wake up now?

March 18, 2021

Nocturne

O Shepherd of

Dreams

wanderer or the night,
assemblage
shape
nimble,
time

in

the forest of
darkness

Teach us

the density of meaning

quilts
beyond language:

wild longing?

the blurry lines in between

MARCH 31, 2021

Nocturne

O shepherd of
dreams,
wanderer of the night,
assemblage
shape
nimble
time,
in
the forest of
darkness,

teach us
the density of meaning,

quilts
beyond language:

—wild longing?—

the blurry lines in between.

March 31, 2021

Advice for an
insomniac

"What day is it?

"What time is it?"

What's your emergency?

looking up at night,

let the question hang in the air

inhabit

time,

go

wake up

God

APRIL 21, 2021

Advice for an Insomniac

What day is it?

What time is it?

What's your emergency?

Looking up at night,

let the question hang in the air,

inhabit time.

Go

wake up

God!

April 21, 2021

words feel insufficient here

words often fail.

maps
journeying through it

tiresome quicksand .

As someone who has spent too much time thinking

I'm drawn to
silence

in dialogue with

Dreams

MARCH 29, 2021

Words Feel Insufficient Here

Words often fail,

maps

journeying through it,

tiresome quicksand;

as someone who has spent too much time thinking,

I'm drawn to

silence

in dialogue with

dreams.

March 29, 2021

taking a **word** for a walk

Humor
unleash-
ing deep melancholy from the inside out.

intimacy with the dreadful

bedlam — bellowed

"Like grunts, howls,

shrieks."

— a seem-
ingly random, disordered and complex
process —

What will happen next is not clear

Order Amid Disorder

the evolu tion of language

"It would be meaningless for an animal to
produce a fre- quency that can't be heard

MARCH 9, 2021

Taking a Word for a Walk

Humor
unleashing
deep melancholy from the inside out,
intimacy with the dreadful
bedlam – bellowed,
like grunts, howls, shrieks
— a seemingly
random, disordered and complex
process –
what will happen next is not clear:
order amid disorder,
the evolution of language.
It would be meaningless for an animal
to produce a frequency that can't be heard.

March 9, 2021

Listen

[Writing is] a way of

deep listening

sentience itself

Thick strokes of

thought,
in the moment,

intimate and vulnerable

peel
off layers of

someone else's howling,

like an autopsy

APRIL 5, 2021

Listen

Writing is a way of
deep listening,
sentience itself;
thick strokes of
thought
in the moment,
intimate and vulnerable.
Peel
off layers of
someone else's howling
like an autopsy.

April 5, 2021

Lethal

Still, life

Beyond the fleeting

right now?
what
here?

— turbulent yet
at the root
most revelatory

Time

captured the exact

unrestrained chaos

applied to the paper surface

Like it's

someone else's

zoo

MARCH 21, 2021

Lethal
Still Life

Beyond the fleeting

—right now?

What,

here?

—turbulent yet

at the root

most revelatory—

time

captured the exact

unrestrained chaos,

applied to the paper surface

like it's

someone else's

zoo.

March 21, 2021

**field recordings of bird
song.**

vessel of voices

Bird with a
mournful cry

shrieks, mews, moans, whoops, ululations,

giggle like a loon,

MAY 9, 2021

Field Recordings of Bird Song

Vessel of voices,
bird with a mournful cry,
shrieks, mews, moans, whoops, ululations,
giggle like a loon.

May 9, 2021

POETRY

I didn't sit down to write a poem

There's so much to be mined

love, vengeance, madness
                    prophecy,
            secrets and lies

                sound bellowing from some-
one's throat

                        I'm not go-
ing to dwell on stuff that's going to break my
heart.

at the end of the day, all

you have to do is lie

artfully

                You can do this. Keep
going.

APRIL 1, 2021

Poetry

I didn't sit down to write a poem.
There's so much to be mined:
love, vengeance, madness,
prophecy,
secrets and lies
—sound bellowing from some-
one's throat—
I'm not going
to dwell on stuff that's going to break
my heart.
At the end of the day, all
you have to do is lie
artfully.
You can do this.
Keep going.

April 1, 2021

ode to
nothing
time

Even if you choose
to do nothing, you can do it with
intensity.

wonderfully visceral

small improvisations

My routine is to not
have a routine."

stop thinking

represent
recitation
sex.
riff
Rime

To please, seduce, divert,
enchant; I feel that I have only
ever lived for this.

I'm not going to lie

Basically,

I

just like

playing.

MARCH 16, 2021

Ode to
Nothing
Time

Even if you choose
to do nothing, you can
do it with intensity:
wonderfully visceral
small improvisations,
my routine
is to not have a routine;
stop thinking,
represent,
recitation,
sex,
riff
rime;
to please, seduce, divert, enchant,
I feel
that I have only ever lived for this.
I'm not going to lie,
basically I
just like
playing.

March 16, 2021

THE TELLING

Holding
your breath and speaking tele-
pathically

"I am
the text

of

a story
austere

drawn on scraps of paper, or
someone else's stationery —

Artifice

scraped
                    raw
down.
to the ordinary,

APRIL 19, 2021

The Telling

Holding
your breath and speaking
telepathically,

I am
the text
of
a story
austere
drawn on scraps of paper, or
someone else's stationery –

artifice
scraped
raw
down
to the ordinary.

April 19, 2021

WEDNESDAY's   wisdom

Call it a ghost

inhabiting the
the face of it,

the face of a   younger self

like a mirror for

the future

no longer imaginable,

faces
age

and the long shadow

the forces we cannot see

we tell ourselves stories

sketches, songs, monologues

tell ourselves other people's stories in order
to form our own.

That image has reverberated

It was almost thrown out in the trash.

MARCH 10, 2021

Wednesday's wisdom

Call it a ghost
inhabiting
the face of it,
face of a younger self
like a mirror
for the future
no longer imaginable;
faces
age,
and the long shadow,
the forces we cannot see;
we tell ourselves stories,
sketches, songs, monologues,
tell ourselves other people's stories
in order to form our own;
that image has reverberated,
it was almost thrown out in the trash.

March 10, 2021

Who I see in the mirror

A resigned half smile played on his lips
as he talked, as if he recognized the futility

forced
to be alone with myself,

"My face was basically falling off,"

The big eyes and gaping

mouth

him
turned,
It

to illustrate the letter "I."

I live it.

But how do the worms know to do this?

I wonder

MARCH 12, 2021

Who I See in the Mirror

A resigned half-smile played on his lips
as he talked, as if he recognized the futility;
forced
to be alone with myself,
my face was basically falling off,
the big eyes and gaping
mouth:
him
turned
it,
to illustrate the letter "i"
I live it.
But how do the worms know to do this?
I wonder.

March 12, 2021

Reinventing himself

I have always wanted to explore another
                                        I

Untaught, untamed

terminal.
cartoonish

she

him,
you,
lots of
        it

seems to fluctuate a bit,

blue eyes gone gray,

designing myself,

an echo and an ancestor.

APRIL 7, 2021

Reinventing Himself

I have always wanted to explore another
I;
untaught, untamed,
terminal
cartoonish,

she,
him,
you,
lots of
it,
seems to fluctuate a bit,

blue eyes gone gray,
designing myself,

an echo and an ancestor.

April 7, 2021

self in ... h ... rubble
of Yuka R... ree
"At that moment

Not many vic
to sustain a solic
men ... never
perception as a
brigh ...oned, assu

... and
...ared her summer cot
tage find their lives thrown into
gloom and disrepair
surrender, Dorothy" Meg Wo-
litzer's slender new novel, tells the
story of the aftermath of Sara's
ath. It follows the vapor trails left
the lives of Natalie Swe... low,
entered, di-
am L...ger
a's insepa
fidant. Ad
is also
ing when
is despe
lso in t
eter a la
...cher amb
e parents o
med Dunca
...ighly a... mature
...s who surround
more aimless
se previous

...o
...es — j
...ven ... halfhe
the floating
for ...very
it is one

...way
...ys and em
...t day stuffed
and seething
Sara dies b...
...ick excur

...rely. But it
s. Wolitzer's story takes
...ally undernourished ...ut
...orld it evokes. Surr
...y" retains its lean
righ to the end, ...n
...ree of resolution
...ters who

APRIL 7, 1999

Self in Rubble

Not many
sustain
perception;
thrown into
gloom and disrepair,
the aftermath
vapor
trails,
aimless,
floating,
seething,
undernourished
to the end.

April 7, 1999

postscript

writing fugitive lines in the air

the shadows of things

don't search for an aesthetic,

just getting the words out

MARCH 22, 2021

Postscript

writing fugitive lines in the air

the shadows of things

don't search for an aesthetic

just getting the words out

March 22, 2021

Acknowledgments

Among the many inspirations for these cutups are the pressed hand prints of prehistoric cave dwellers, recycled fragments of 10th century Japanese calligraphers, Tristan Tzara's textual experiments, Max Jacob's prose poems, or what he called his "mots en liberté" (words on the loose), Kurt Schwitters' mixed media and verbal collages, David Bowie's song lyrics, and my Kindergarten teacher Miss Derwick, who first taught me how to wield a pair of scissors. Thanks to my daughter, Aurélie, son, Jacques, and brother, Harold, for teaching me the rudiments of Photoshop. Special thanks to Harold for his cover design and to my friend Jean-Luc Fievert for the author's photo. And as always, thanks to my wonderful publisher, Mark Givens, who gets it.

"Self in Rubble," "Advice for an Insomniac," and "Words Feel Insufficient Here," were first published in *Unlost, an online journal of found poetry and art.*

BAMBOO DART PRESS

112 N. Harvard Ave. #65
Claremont, CA 91711

chapbooks@bamboodartpress.com
www.bamboodartpress.com

www.ingramcontent.com/pod-product-compliance
Lightning Source LLC
Chambersburg PA
CBHW081241020426
42331CB00013B/3256